yo June, a shakespeare buff
Merry Christ
(

Shakespeare's Guide
to Parenting

JAMES ANDREWS

DEY ST.
AN IMPRINT OF
WILLIAM MORROW *PUBLISHERS*

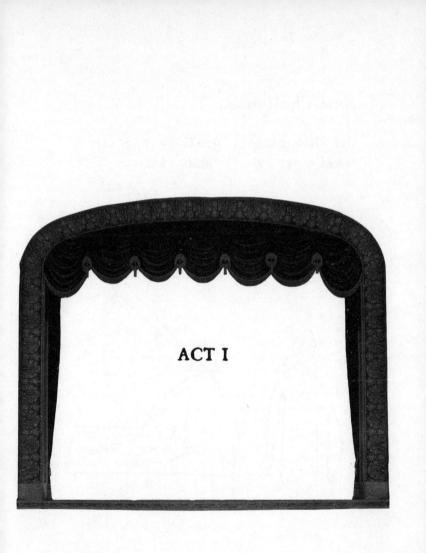

ACT I

New Challenges

As new parents you'll face fresh challenges on a daily basis:

The Taming of the Shrew: II, i

It's vital that at least one of you maintains a sense of perspective:

Why do you make such faces? When all's done you look but on a stool.

Macbeth: III, iv

Loss of Sleep

Sleep deprivation is one of the few things that new parents can do little to prepare themselves for:

It's also one of those problems that seldom just goes away:

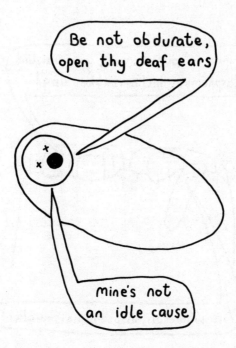

Be not obdurate, open thy deaf ears

mine's not an idle cause

Titus Andronicus: II, iii

Othello: I, ii

Try calling out to them, they may just need the reassurance of hearing your voice;

The Tempest: 1, i

though, ultimately, one of you may need to get up:

Henry VI Part 1: V, iv

Crying

It's important not to be
intimidated by a crying baby...

Love's Labours Lost : III, i

As You Like It : II, v

though, equally, it would be naive
not to accept that there are
going to be some dark times
ahead:

Henry VI Part 1 : V, iv

Calming Your Baby

A crying baby can sometimes be pacified by being played with or tossed about, but be careful...

The Tempest: II, ii

...not to attempt this too soon after a feeding:

King John: IV, iii

Breast Feeding

If you've decided to breast feed you'll know that babies want feeding at the most inconvenient times:

King Lear: I, iv

Even so, you'll need to secure
a certain level of privacy if
you want to avoid becoming
part of the general conversation:

Hamlet: II, ii

Coriolanus: I, iii

Getting Back To Normal

There's no reason why a month or two after the birth you shouldn't be back to enjoying a normal, healthy sex-life;

King Lear: I, i

though this is something that
you may wish to discuss with
your partner:

Much Ado About Nothing: IV, ii

Hamlet: IV, v

Early Talkers

A baby taking his first tentative steps into the world of speech can at times present as a bit of a nuisance:

The Merry Wives of Windsor: I, iv

Twelfth Night: IV, ii

Gently suggesting that he may wish to desist is the obvious way forward, ...

King Lear: III, vi

Troilus and Cressida: V, i

... though you may ultimately need to enlist the help of a family member:

Take the boy to you: he so troubles me, 'tis past enduring

The Winter's Tale: II, i

Widen the palate

Encouraging your child to try new and exotic foods from an early age can help to prevent fussy eating habits later on.

Antony and Cleopatra: V, ii

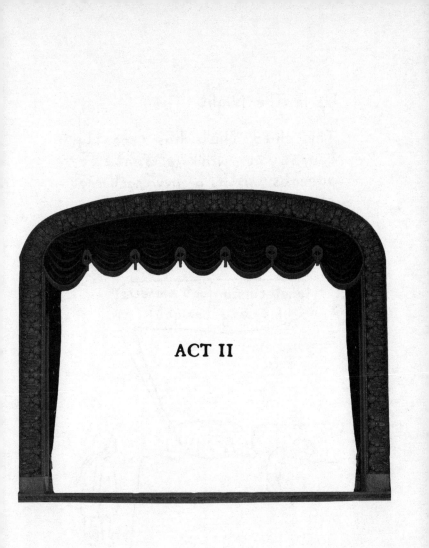

ACT II

Up In The Night

The child that has recently learnt to walk presents parents with a new nocturnal challenge,

Romeo and Juliet: V, iii

and often comes armed with
a store of unlikely excuses:

Didst thou not hear a noise?

I have the toothache

I find not myself
disposed to sleep

Macbeth: II, ii

Much Ado About Nothing: III, ii

The Tempest: II, i

23

Insisting on your 'right to rest' is vital if you want to continue to offer a high level of care:

Antony and Cleopatra : IV, xxii

The Demanding Child

Some children can be incredibly demanding, even at a young age:

The Winter's Tale : IV, iv

Don't allow yourself to be
dictated to by such a child,

Fair one, I think not so

All's Well That Ends Well: II, iii

and be prepared to suffer the hurt of unkind words:

The Merry Wives of Windsor: I,i

Henry IV Part 1: II,iv

The Tempest: II,i

Supermarket Tantrums

Lots has been written about supermarket tantrums but one of the simplest techniques is still one of the best:

> No part of it is mine; this shame derives itself from unknown loins

Much Ado About Nothing: IV.i

The Importance Of Quiet-times

Bringing up children can be an exhausting business - don't feel guilty about insisting on a bit of peace and quiet once in a while:

King Lear: I, iv

King Lear: V, iii

Keep It Serious

Being laughed at by a three year-old while administering a rebuke is a clear taint on your authority, and will need to be answered:

Henry VI Part 1: II, iii

Dealing With Hatred

Being told that you're hated is an unfortunate but almost inevitable part of parenting:

Be certain. Nothing truer—'tis no jest that I do hate thee

A Midsummer Night's Dream: III, ii

Giving some advance thought to how you might respond may ease an otherwise distressing interchange:

We hate alike. Not Afric owns a serpent I abhor more

Coriolanus: I, viii

Maintain A Firm Stance

Refuse to countenance crass attempts at regaining your favour.

The Tempest: I, ii

the more so when the fall
from favour has been great:

Vile thing, let loose,
or I will shake thee from
me like a serpent

A Midsummer Night's Dream: III,ii

Avoid Rash Sanctions

When you're faced with behaviour that needs to be challenged don't be too hasty to hand out a sanction. Take your time...

Titus Andronicus: II, iii

... you might come up with something you wouldn't otherwise have thought of:

This is our doom

Thou shalt be whipped with wire and stewed in brine, smarting in lingering pickle!

Titus Andronicus: V, iii

Antony and Cleopatra: II, v

Mum, mum!

king Lear: I, iv

Avoiding The 'No' Word

Try to avoid becoming one of those parents who's forever saying 'No' to things, there are alternatives:

Fair one, I think not so

It is most retrograde to our desire

All's Well That Ends Well: II, iii

Hamlet: I, ii

Stoicism

Introducing your child to philosophy at a young age can help them come to terms with difficult concepts such as loss and bereavement:

Julius Caesar: II,ii

A Death In The Family

The death of a much-loved family pet may provoke some difficult questions:

The Taming of the Shrew: IV, i

As grown-ups it will fall to you to find the appropriate words:

His cares are now all ended

He's walked the way of nature, and to our purposes he lives no more

Henry IV Part 2: V, ii

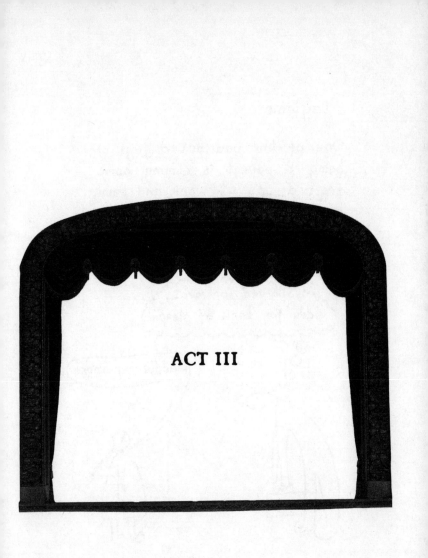

ACT III

Playtime

One of the undisputed joys of being a parent is coming home from a day at work and being met at the door by someone who just wants to play:

The Taming of the Shrew: IV, iii

Richard II: V, ii

Graciously accept the role given
you in these play episodes...

I was not made a horse,
and yet I bear a burden
like an ass

Richard II : V, v

...and be prepared to go the extra mile:

Richard II : III, iii

Safety At Home

A good parent tries to see accidents before they happen. If that's not one of your parental giftings, however...

[Enter Juliet somewhat fast]

Romeo and Juliet: II,vi

...try to see them at the
earliest opportunity after:

Romeo and Juliet: II, iii

Monitoring Sweet Intake

Keep a close eye on what your child is eating between meals and take steps to ensure that they don't ruin their appetite:

king Lear: III, vii

Table Manners

Try to instil a basic level of table etiquette, such as not starting until everyone has been served:

Antony and Cleopatra : II, ii

In The Car

Appealing to the better nature of children on long car journeys may prove a bootless task:

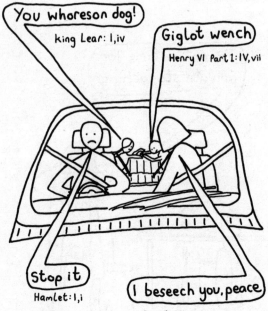

History has shown that the back of a hairbrush has often succeeded where words have failed:

Henry VI Part 1: IV, i

Respecting Danger

Children should be encouraged to develop a healthy respect for the potential dangers of everyday life:

The Merry Wives of Windsor: I,i

The Taming of the Shrew: IV,i

The fact that disobedience may result in serious physical harm is, however, something that your child may need to learn for himself:

To wilful men, the injuries that they themselves procure must be their schoolmasters

King Lear: II, iv

Listening To Your Child

A child that has suffered an injustice at the hands of his contemporaries needs to be heard:

Macbeth: V, v

Take steps to discourage tale-telling, however, and don't be too hasty to accept the version of events given:

It is a tale told by an idiot, full of sound and fury, signifying nothing

Macbeth: V, v

Hobbies and Interests

Take an active involvement in your child's hobbies and interests, recognising that there may be some personal costs attached to this:

I do smell all horse-piss

The Tempest: IV, i

Musicianship

A child with a gift for music should be encouraged, though the reverse may apply to those from whom the gift has been withheld:

A Midsummer Night's Dream: V, i

The Taming of the Shrew: III, i

Being honest with them about their limitations is a good way of forestalling future disappointment...

The Two Gentlemen of Verona: IV, ii

Timon of Athens: I, ii

... but be careful not to appear insensitive to the feelings of even the most fledgling of musical prodigies:

> And with that word she struck me on the head, and through the instrument my pate made way

The Taming of the Shrew : II, i

Praise, Praise, Praise

There's a lot been written about the importance of praise when it comes to parenting – make sure you're getting enough:

Praise him that got thee...

...she that gave thee suck

Troilus and Cressida: II, iii

Dealing with Verbal Abuse

Children can at times be brutally unkind:

King Lear : II, ii

Remain calm and objective. Try to identify the underlying issues that may have led to the outburst...

Hamlet : III.iv

...remembering all the while that a serious affront may require a physical response:

Come, recreant. Come, thou child, I'll whip thee with a rod

A Midsummer Night's Dream: III, ii

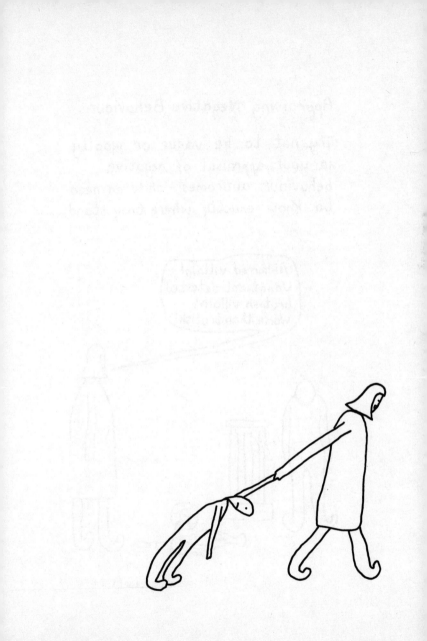

Appraising Negative Behaviour

Try not to be vague or woolly in your appraisal of negative behaviour outcomes - children need to know exactly where they stand:

King Lear: I, ii

Taking Responsibility

When encountering negative behaviour be sure to give a clear voice to your sense of disappointment, even if it means taking some personal responsibility:

Richard III : 1, iii

Getting An Apology

After a falling-out always provide your child with an opportunity to say sorry.

Macbeth: III, i

Antony and Cleopatra: I, i

...remembering that a couple of mumbled words is no guarantee of a repentant spirit:

Macbeth: II, iii

King John: IV, iii

Siblings In League

If you have more than one child you may find that they occasionally form highly unlikely and very annoying co-operatives:

Richard III: I,iv

Henry VI Part 2: III,ii

Be quick to realise when one of your edicts is being challenged by one of these temporary alliances...

May it please you, noble madam, to withdraw...

O inglorious league!

Henry VIII: III, i

King John: V, i

...and demonstrate a firm intent
not to discuss the matter further:

Thy brother by decree is banishèd:
If thou dost bend and pray and
fawn for him, I spurn thee like
a cur out of my way

Julius Caesar: III, i

You may wish to seal your resolution with a mild oath:

Away! By Jupiter, this shall not be revoked!

King Lear: 1, i

Defend Your Prerogatives

In a world where the voice of young people is becoming increasingly powerful you may sometimes need to remind your children who it is that makes the decisions:

Inform yourselves we need no more of your advice

Our prerogative calls not your counsels

The Winter's Tale: II, i

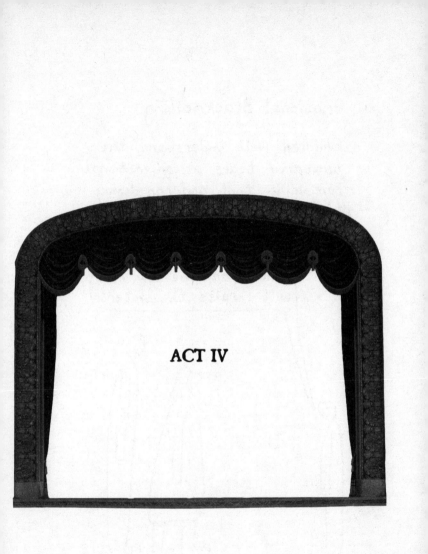

ACT IV

Emotional Blackmailing

Children well understand the power of tears as an emotional bargaining tool, and can deploy them at will if sufficiently compromised:

The Merchant of Venice: II, ii

Be careful not to fall victim
to this kind of emotional
blackmailing:

Trust not those cunning
waters of his eyes, for villainy
is not without such rheum

King John : IV, iii

... that you shouldn't benefit from a little emotional blackmailing of your own:

O monstrous! What reproachful words are these?

Titus Andronicus : I, i

May this be borne?

Titus Andronicus : IV, iv

Mine eyes smell onions

All's Well That Ends Well : V, iii

Terms Of Reproach

Be on your guard for previously unheard-of terms of reproach:

Troilus and Cressida: V,i and II,i

What may at first appear as a relatively mild form of abuse may in fact be the very latest in street vulgarity:

Love's Labour's Lost: IV, i

The Merry Wives of Windsor: III, i

Expectation Management

Christmas and birthdays can be a difficult time financially speaking. Encouraging your child to self-manage their expectations can lead to significant savings:

Youngling, learn thou to make some meaner choice

Titus Andronicus: II, i

Shop Shaming

A trip to the shops with the children can end up being a humiliating affair:

Henry VI Part 1: I, iv

Ensure that the affected party has a say in however you decide to proceed...

Much Ado About Nothing: V, i

... and try to resolve the incident in such a way that there are no lasting feelings of bitterness:

All's Well That Ends Well: V, iii

Much Ado About Nothing: V, i

School Refusers

Most children go through a stage of not wanting to go to school. The key to getting them through this is to remain positive at all times:

> Then the whining schoolboy, with his satchel and shining morning face, creeping like snail unwillingly to school

As You Like It : II, vii

Group Punishments

Group punishments are an excellent way of delivering quick, easy and effective justice, though accusations of miscarriages may sometimes be alleged:

Be it known that we the greatest are misthought for things that others do

Antony and Cleopatra: V, ii

Be able to demonstrate sound
legal reasoning behind all your
rulings:

Antony and Cleopatra: V, ii

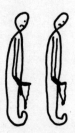

Sanctions

Be wary of rashly administering a sanction that you may later lack the resolve to see through. Remember, excellent outcomes can be achieved through epic-sounding yet non-specific threats:

I will have such revenges on you both that all the world shall - I will do such things - what they are I know not; but they shall be the terrors of the earth

King Lear: II, iv

Smacking

There's no doubt that smacking isn't as popular as it used to be. An extreme sense of personal violation, however, may still demand a physical response:

You shall know, my boys, your mother's hand shall right your mother's wrong

Titus Andronicus: II, iii

Beware of sophisticated arguments
designed to distract you from
the matter at hand...

Julius Caesar: II, i

The Merchant of Venice: IV, I

... and have in place some well-reasoned arguments of your own:

King Lear: II, ii

Miscarriages Of Justice

As a parent you're only human so it's possible you'll get the odd decision wrong from time to time:

The Two Gentlemen of Verona: IV, iv

An improvised homily touching the precarious and transient nature of innocence may help:

Thou knowest in the state of innocency Adam fell...

Henry IV Part 1 : III,iii

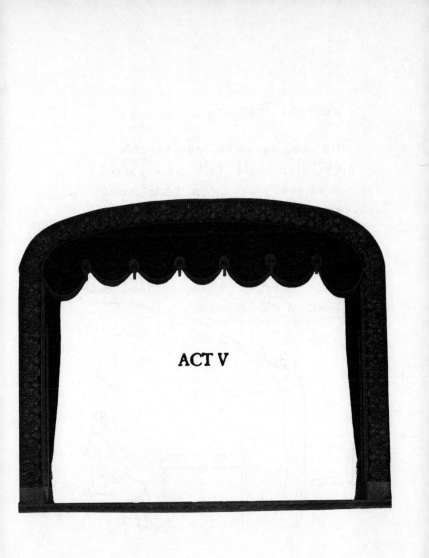

ACT V

Parents' Evening

As anyone with adolescent children will tell you, parents' evenings can be a chastening experience:

From forth the kennel of thy womb hath crept a hellhound that doth hunt us all to death

Richard III : IV, iv

As a parent you'll need to take responsibility for the actions of your child, but only up to a point:

He is my son - yea, and therein my shame; yet from my dugs he drew not this deceit

Richard III: II, ii

Support your position with any other
excuses that you can call to mind.

Good wombs have
borne bad sons

The Tempest: I, ii

Academic Attainment:

School report time is an excellent opportunity for a frank appraisal of your child's education:

Othello: V, ii

Giving voice to your sense of disappointment can be an excellent way of driving up standards:

King Lear: I, i

Family Mealtimes

Eating together is an important part of family life so don't allow these get-togethers to be compromised by foul or unseemly behaviour:

[A trumpet sounds]

There let him stand and rave and cry for food...

Titus Andronicus: V, iii

Show that you're prepared to take a very firm line on this:

... If anyone relieves or pities him, for the offence he dies

Titus Andronicus: V, iii

Fussy Eaters

Fussy eaters can be a real pain:

Twelfth Night: IV, i

If your child continues to be particular about their food explain in no uncertain terms what the alternative will be:

Titus Andronicus: IV, ii

A teenage son that is the very reverse of fussy, however, may pose a problem of a very different kind:

The devil speed him! No man's pie is freed from his ambitious finger

Henry VIII: I, i

Table Wars

Don't allow mealtimes to turn into a battle of wills:

Henry V : V, i

Timon of Athens : IV, iii

Allow your child the right not to like certain foods, and have suitable alternatives on hand:

How say you to a fat tripe finely broiled?

The Taming of the Shrew: IV, iii

Rebranding

When it comes to food some children will be fussy for fussy's sake. Giving a new name to an old meal may help:

The Merchant of Venice: II, vii

Troilus and Cressida: I, ii

Alternatively, you may feel it's time to add something new to the menu:

The Taming of the Shrew: IV, i

The Winter's Tale: IV, iv

Dealing With Ungratefulness

Despite your best endeavours not everything that you provide for your dependant will be met with the anticipated level of appreciation:

King Lear: III, iii

Be open and honest about how this makes you feel:

King Lear: I, iv

Providing them with an opportunity to reflect independently on the many sacrifices you make on their behalf may be a good way of moving forward:

King Lear: 1, i

Teenage Daughters

A teenage daughter can be a real worry, particularly come Friday night:

O shame, where is thy blush?

Hamlet: III, iv

Try to impress upon her the importance of encouraging the right
kind of male attention...

A golden mind stoops
not to shows of dross

The Merchant of Venice: II, vii

... understanding all the while that your daughter may choose to reject your good counsel.

Men's eyes were made to look, and let them gaze...

...by my heel I care not.

Romeo and Juliet: III, i

General Unpleasantness

As the parent of a teenage daughter you could be forgiven for thinking that some of their rudeness is just a little bit unnecessary:

King Lear: I, iv

The Two Gentlem of Verona: IV, iv

Offer a reminder of the father daughter relationship as it exists in popular tradition

Be advised, fair maid: to you your father should be as a god

A Midsummer Night's Dream: 1,i

and try not to be disheartened
if you don't see immediate
results:

Peace, ye fat-guts

Do thou amend thy face,
and I'll amend my life

Henry IV Part 1: II, ii

Henry IV Part 1: III, iii

Sloth

Teenage boys have a particular tendency towards sloth and may need support in observing traditional sleeping and waking patterns:

Romeo and Juliet: IV, v

Richard III: V, iii

Building Bridges

Taking an interest in popular
youth culture can be a good
way of bridging the inter-
generational gap.

Much Ado About Nothing: II, iii

Henry VI Part 2: III, i

... but be realistic about the size of gap that you can reasonably hope to bridge:

HOW DOST THOU LIKE THIS TUNE?

HOW DO YOU, MAN? THE MUSIC LIKES YOU NOT

Twelfth Night: II, iv

The Two Gentlemen of Verona: IV, ii

Unregulated Play

Episodes of unregulated play can quickly degenerate into behaviour that needs to be challenged:

The Merchant of Venice: I, i

If you can't negotiate an improvement in behaviour per se, try to broker an agreement regarding its precise location:

Twelfth Night: IV, i

Dangerous Play

Boys can be particularly thought-
less when it comes to the
consequences of dangerous play:

Hamlet: V, ii

Oversympathising may not be the answer, and could even be seen as an affirmation of risky behaviour.

Richard III : IV, ii

Antony and Cleopatra : I, ii

Dealing With Insolence

Be quick to realise when your efforts at reform are not being taken seriously:

King Lear: II,ii

Be prepared to accept the assistance of your partner, they may be able to support you in a way you had not envisaged:

Othello: II, iii

Coping With Regret

Getting a visit from your neighbour about your sons' antisocial behaviour can make for uncomfortable listening...

Titus Andronicus: II, iii

... and may lead to moments
of deep personal regret:

Richard III: II, ii

Henry IV Part 2 : IV, iii

Don't be too quick to blame yourself. If you're struggling with this look to your partner for some words of support:

Good wombs have borne bad sons

The Tempest: I.ii

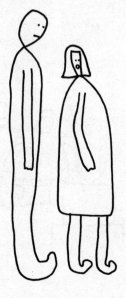

Oratory

Do not underestimate the power of a finely worded, well rehearsed speech:

Check thy contempt. Obey our will which travails in thy good. Believe not thy disdain, but presently do thine own fortunes that obedient right which both thy duty owes and our power claims; or I will throw thee from my care forever into the staggers and the careless lapse of youth and ignorance.

All's Well That Ends Well: II, iii

Published by arrangement with Vintage Publishers,
a division of the Random House Group Limited.

HarperCollins books may be purchased for educational, business, or sales
promotional use. For information, please e-mail the Special Markets
Department at SPsales@harpercollins.com.

A hardcover edition of this book was published in 2015 by Square Peg,
an imprint of Vintage, Penguin Random House U.K.

FIRST DEY STREET BOOKS EDITION PUBLISHED 2015.

Library of Congress Cataloging-in-Publication Data has been applied for.

ISBN 978-0-06-244250-5

15 16 17 18 19 OV/RRD 10 9 8 7 6 5 4 3 2 1